LIVING WITH
Others

A WORKBOOK FOR STEPS 8–12

Created by James Hubal and Joanne Hubal

Based on material from *A Program for You: A Guide to the Big Book's* Design for Living* published by Hazelden Publishing

Hazelden
Publishing

---

*BIG BOOK is a registered trademark of Alcoholics Anonymous World Services, Inc.; used here with permission of AAWS.

Hazelden Publishing
Center City, MN 55012
hazelden.org/bookstore

ISBN: 978-1-568-38991-2

Editor's note:

Hazelden Publishing offers a variety of information on addiction
and related areas. Our publications do not necessarily represent
the Hazelden Betty Ford Foundation's programs, nor do they
officially speak for any Twelve Step organization.

The Twelve Steps and Twelve Traditions are reprinted and adapted
with permission of Alcoholics Anonymous World Services, Inc.
Permission to reprint and adapt the Twelve Steps does not mean
that Alcoholics Anonymous has reviewed or approved the contents of
this publication, nor that AA agrees with the views expressed herein.
The views expressed herein are solely those of the authors. AA is
a program of recovery from alcoholism. Use of the Twelve Steps in
connection with programs and activities that are patterned after AA,
but which address other problems, does not imply otherwise.

This workbook has been updated to include both third-
and fourth-edition page references to *Alcoholics Anonymous*.

Cover and interior design/typesetting: Sara Streifel, *Think Creative Design*
Developmental editor: Marc Olson
Editorial project manager: Victoria Tirrel

Contents

Introduction

The book *Alcoholics Anonymous,* commonly known as the Big Book, is the basic text for the fellowship of Alcoholics Anonymous (AA). It was published in 1939 to show how the first one hundred or so AA members found recovery from alcoholism. The founders of AA were Bill W., a New York stockbroker, and Dr. Bob, an Akron, Ohio, physician. Bill W. wrote the Big Book with the help of Dr. Bob and the other early members. He wrote the first 164 pages in a specific order that has not been changed or reworded since 1939. He wrote these pages so that if other alcoholics read the suggestions for recovery and put them into practice in exactly the order Bill W. wrote them, they would find recovery too.

Since 1939 millions of alcoholics and, more recently, countless people suffering from other addictive behaviors have done just that—they have found recovery.

This program of recovery is not a philosophy or religion. It is a practical *design for living* that is summed up in the Twelve suggestions, or Steps, listed on pages 59–60 of the Big Book and on page 40 at the back of this workbook. If you aren't familiar with the Twelve Steps, you should read them through carefully now.

———

The first three Steps show us how we can build a working relationship with our Higher Power, or God *as we understand God.* Steps One, Two, and Three are covered in the Big Book from page xxiii [xxv, 4th ed.] to the bottom of page 63. The next four Steps—Steps Four through Seven—show us how we can better know and live at peace with ourselves. Steps Four, Five, Six, and Seven are covered in the Big Book from the last two lines of page 63 through the end of the second paragraph on page 76. Finally, the last five Steps—Steps Eight through Twelve—give us a design for living meaningful lives with

Duplicating this page is illegal. Do not copy this material without written permission from the publisher.

1

other people and for continuing a daily program of recovery the rest of our lives. The Big Book covers these Steps from the third paragraph on page 76 to the end of page 103.

This workbook addresses Steps Eight through Twelve and is the third of three workbooks covering all Twelve Steps. All three workbooks were written to help you study the Big Book and apply what it says. Much of the text in these workbooks is adapted from the book *A Program for You: A Guide to the Big Book's Design for Living,* written anonymously by two AA old-timers. You will benefit even more from these workbooks if you first read that book.*

While *A Program for You* is an optional supplement to these workbooks, a copy of the Big Book, *Alcoholics Anonymous,* is not—it is essential. Everything you need to know to be on the road to recovery from alcoholism (or another addiction) is in the Big Book. Anything else, including these workbooks, can only help you see what is already in the Big Book as you apply its suggestions in your life.

––––––

The Big Book and the fellowship of Alcoholics Anonymous are both concerned only with recovery from addiction to the drug alcohol. Neither the Big Book nor the fellowship makes any claim for what the suggestions in the Big Book will do for people other than alcoholics. Therefore, when referring to the Big Book or the AA fellowship, we will use the terms "alcohol" and "alcoholics."

Since the Big Book was written, many successful Twelve Step groups for recovery from other addictions and addictive behaviors have been established—Al-Anon, Cocaine Anonymous, Narcotics Anonymous, Overeaters Anonymous, and so on. While these groups publish their own literature, their basic program for recovery is not essentially different from the one described in AA's Big Book. In this workbook, when referring to recovery in general, or to you, the reader, we will use a variety of terms and references to include those who are not addicted specifically or exclusively to alcohol.

––––––––––––

A Program For You: A Guide to the Big Book's Design for Living is published by and available through Hazelden Publishing.

A Design for Living

By this time you have begun to see some changes in your life. You have worked hard on the first seven Steps, and great things are starting to happen. As you continue to work the Twelve Steps, you'll come to see that the Steps are really *a design for living*. The Twelve Steps are not a process you do once. They're something you bring with you, carry out, and practice day after day.

You can also see that one of the themes of the Big Book is *change* and another is *action*. Once you've successfully completed Steps One through Seven, you've removed the things that blocked you from your Higher Power, and you have found your right relationship with that Power. Being in harmony with your Higher Power means you are ready to live in harmony with other people as well.

Once you're sure you've completed Steps One through Seven honestly and thoroughly, you're ready to put your changes into action. At this point, you have a chance to set things right with your fellow human beings. You are ready for Steps Eight and Nine.

> Stop here and open your Big Book. Read from the third paragraph on page 76 to the end of line 15 on page 84.

My Eighth Step

Here is the Eighth Step in the AA Twelve Step program:

**"Made a list of all persons we had harmed,
and became willing to make amends to them all."**

Notice that this Step has two parts: first, make a list of persons harmed; second, become willing to make amends. Let's begin with the first part: making a list.

Making a list of the people you've harmed should be easy if you've thoroughly followed the Big Book's directions. Most of the people's names are probably on the lists you made in Step Four. Use the information on the personal inventories you've already done to fill in the lists on the upcoming pages for this Step.

If you've used another method to complete your Fourth Step inventory, you may now need to list the names of all the people you've harmed by the wrongs, defects of character, and shortcomings you've admitted, written down, and turned over in Steps Four through Seven.

> First, write on a separate piece of paper the names of all the people you've listed on your Step Four inventory—the people you've harmed—and add any names that may have somehow been left out.
>
> In exercises 1–4, you'll take this complete list of people and break it down into four smaller lists.

The first list you'll make, on the next page, will be of the names of people you're willing to make amends to right away. These are people who will be the easiest for you to approach. We'll call this first list of names the *Now List*.

Because this list, and the three lists that follow it, are ones you actually intend to use, after each name, write the information you'll need to get in touch with that person. If you don't know someone's name, address, email address, or phone number, write in the last column on the right the name of someone who could help you get that information.

It is important to remember that the contact information on the list is only to help you reach the person to set up a face-to-face meeting. It means you'll have everything you need to move ahead when the time comes. It does *not* mean that writing an email or letter or making a phone call will take the place of seeing the person you've harmed in person. That meeting must happen if at all possible.

Go to the next page and complete your Now List, which will consist of the names of people you're willing to contact right away in order to make amends. Use extra paper if you need more room to write.

MY NOW LIST

Name	Address, Email, and/or Phone Number	Who Could Help Me Find This Person?

My Sooner or Later List

Now it is time to write list 2. Let's call this list the *Sooner or Later List.* Here you'll write the names of people you may not feel you can talk to now about the harms you've done, but you know you'll talk to them sooner or later.

Fill in the names and information on the Sooner or Later List as you did on the Now List. (Use more paper if needed.)

LIST 2
MY SOONER OR LATER LIST

Name	Address, Email, and/or Phone Number	Who Could Help Me Find This Person?

Next comes list 3, called the *Maybe List,* where you will list people you're not sure you can ever make amends to.

Fill in this list the same way you did the other two, including the people's addresses and phone numbers wherever possible. (Use more paper if needed.)

LIST 3
MY MAYBE LIST

Name	Address, Email, and/or Phone Number	Who Could Help Me Find This Person?

My Never List

Finally, on list 4, write the names of people you feel you'll never make amends to. This list will be called the *Never List*. (Use more paper if needed.)

Notice that the last column on the right has become a space for you to write why you feel you can never make amends to each person on the list. After you've worked through your first three lists, you'll probably see the information in this column in a new light.

LIST 4

MY NEVER LIST

Name	Address, Email, and/or Phone Number	Why I Can Never Make Amends

The second part of Step Eight says that you must become willing to make amends to all of the people on your list—no matter which list they're on. What might stop you from being willing to make amends? You have given reasons on your Never List, but what do you think some of the other people you need to talk to will do, say, think, or feel when you try to make amends?

On the chart on the next page, write one name from each of these lists: Sooner or Later, Maybe, and Never. Next to each name you'll see the outline of a stop sign. Inside that outline, write what you think might stop you from going to see that person.

Some possible reasons are:

- You hate the person.

- You are divorced from the person.

- You think she will call the cops.

- You owe him money.

- You would be embarrassed.

- You feel they hurt you so badly that you don't owe them anything.

- You don't want to talk about your recovery program.

- You don't want to get into an argument.

> Write nothing in the outlines of the go-ahead arrows to the right of the stop signs. You will return to those in exercise 2 of the next chapter on the Ninth Step. When you're done filling in the stop signs, continue to exercise 6 (page 13).

The Person I Have Harmed	What Stops Me from Going to This Person?	What Encourages Me to Go Ahead

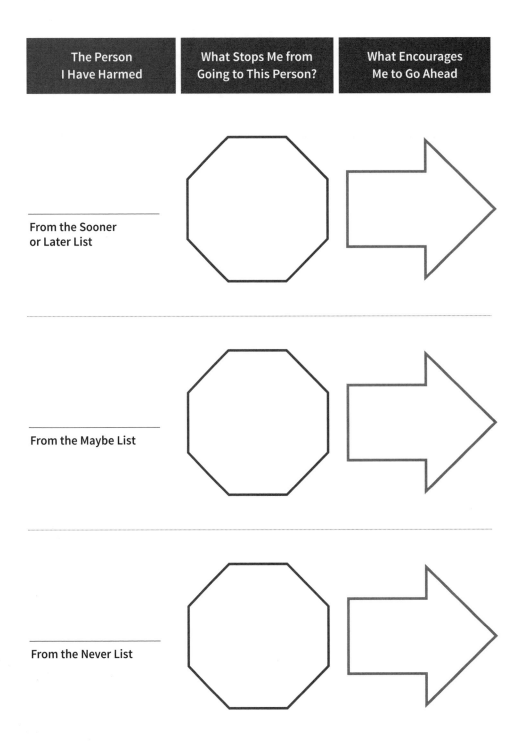

From the Sooner or Later List

From the Maybe List

From the Never List

Here's what you've done so far with Step Eight:

- You've broken down your list of people to whom you have to make amends into four lists in order of difficulty.

- You have a smaller list, written on the stop signs, of some of the things that might stop you from making amends.

- You also know that the second part of Step Eight is to be willing to make amends. Willingness is, in fact, the key to the whole Step. But how can you be willing when making amends is such a difficult thing to do?

> In the Big Book there is a statement that may help you to become willing to make amends. Fill in the rest of the thought below from page 76, lines 24–25, of the Big Book.
>
> **"If we haven't the will to do this** _____
>
> _____**."**

In other words, pray to your Higher Power for willingness and courage until they come. Nowhere in the Big Book does it say you have to make amends to everyone on your lists all at once. It will be a gradual, steady process in which you make amends to one person at a time.

That's why the four separate lists are important. You'll start with the least difficult list (the Now List) and work your way to the hardest (the Never List). If at any time you need more courage, you can pray to your Higher Power and it will come.

When you begin to work with your lists, and as you understand the benefits that come from making amends, you'll become more and more willing to make amends to everyone you've harmed.

With this in mind, you're ready to move along to Step Nine.

My Ninth Step

Here is the Ninth Step in the AA Twelve Step program:

**"Made direct amends to such people wherever possible,
except when to do so would injure them or others."**

The purpose for making amends is to help you get rid of the remorse, fear, and guilt that resulted from hurting people over the years. The Big Book clearly says that the alcoholic or addict needs to make direct amends. In other words, you make your amends face-to-face with people you've harmed. This doesn't mean that amends can never be made over the phone or in a letter, but that more distant options should only be used when a face-to-face meeting is impossible.

There are several benefits of face-to-face contact:

- It opens up compassion and forgiveness in others.

- You will know you have made your best effort.

- You will have made amends in the same way you probably harmed others most—face-to-face.

Exercise 1
More about the Value of Face-to-Face Contact

Unless you meet with someone face-to-face, you're never quite sure you've done your best to make things right with that person. There's something about talking to someone in person that makes things go better, sometimes better than you ever expected.

Think of a time in your life when you had to say something very difficult to another person and when meeting face-to-face made a difference. Maybe you had to say you were sorry or give the person bad news. Describe how being together in person made it more meaningful.

In the next exercise, you'll look at the chart you made on page 12 where, next to each of three names you chose from your lists, you wrote one reason that might keep you from making amends.

Exercise 2
Go-Ahead Arrows

> Read again carefully from line 18 on page 77 through line 13 on page 78 in the Big Book.

You will find you're not alone in worrying about what people will do or say if you try to make amends. A wonderful thing about the Big Book is that the authors have been through what you have and are telling you exactly what worked for them.

> Go back to page 12 and fill in the go-ahead arrows with any answers that have encouraged you to go ahead with your plan to make amends to each person. For example, if you wrote "I hate this person" in the stop sign, in the go-ahead arrow you might write, "I'll go to this person and be as helpful and forgiving as I can. I can admit my bitter feelings and say I regret them."

Like making other kinds of amends, paying back money you owe doesn't have to happen all at once. But you do need to be open and honest about your debts and make specific efforts to repay them if you are to lose your fear of creditors. Otherwise, as the Big Book warns, you'll be liable to drink (or use drugs) again.

The chart on the next page provides a way for you to be specific about how you can repay your debts. Complete your chart as you work out a payment plan with each creditor. (Use more paper if needed.) As soon as you start repaying people, the fear associated with those people and your debts will disappear. Most creditors are happy to work with someone who makes a sincere effort to repay what's owed.

Remember that the Big Book doesn't say you *ought* to lose your fear of creditors; it says you *must* (page 78, line 23).

Person or Institution	Amount Owed	Repayment Schedule (Amount per month, week, etc.)	To Be Paid Off By

The Big Book says we must ask for the strength and direction to make proper amends to everyone we've hurt (see page 79, lines 7–11 in the Big Book). Step Nine states that direct amends be made to people "except when to do so would injure them or others." This might mean not telling someone about something you did to hurt him or her, because the confession might cause the person to be hurt even more. You, with your Higher Power's guidance (which may come through a sponsor, counselor, or trusted friend), will have to be the judge. For those people on your lists who may be further harmed if you admit your wrongs to them, you will admit to yourself and your Higher Power exactly what you've done wrong, and let it go at that.

There are also people on your list who absolutely will not see you or who are impossible to see. The Big Book suggests sending an honest letter in such cases (page 83, lines 22–23).

Write the names of any people on your lists who you think would be hurt if you tried to make amends. Explain how you think each person would be hurt.

Name	How would the person be hurt?

Duplicating this page is illegal. Do not copy this material without written permission from the publisher.

My Ninth Step   19

Write the names of any people on your lists who you definitely feel would not be willing to meet with you. Explain what makes you feel this way.

Name	Why wouldn't the person see you?

Write the names of anyone on your lists who you couldn't see, and explain why. Perhaps the person is dead or living thousands of miles away.

Name	Why couldn't you see this person?

It is important to remember that almost all amends can be made. That means these last three lists shouldn't be very long. With the very few people to whom you'll never be able to make amends face-to-face, it is important to remember that you were willing to do so. Willingness is the key. If they refuse to see you or are physically unavailable to you, you'll know you have honestly done your part. Once you've done what you can with these names you can cross them off your four main lists.

You have now made four lists to use for making amends
(pages 7–10) and a schedule to repay your debts (page 18),
and you've looked in the Big Book, and you've used your
Higher Power's help for an answer to every problem you
thought might stop you from making amends. It is time
now to begin contacting the people on your lists.

MAKING AMENDS

Take another look at the four lists you made, beginning with the
Now List on page 7.

- Make amends to the first person on your Now List, followed
  by the second person, and so forth.

- Make amends to every person on your Now List. By the time
  you've finished, you'll probably be ready to start on your Sooner
  or Later List.

- Do the same thing with your Sooner or Later List (page 8) that
  you did with your first list. Start with the first name on the
  Sooner or Later List, and make amends to that person. Go down
  that list until you've finished.

- When you've finished with the Sooner or Later List, you ought
  to be ready to do your Maybe List (page 9).

- When you've completed your Maybe List, you'll have the courage
  and compassion to go out and make amends to the people you
  thought you'd never be able to face. So go ahead and begin with
  your final list, the Never List (page 10). Make amends to each
  of the people on this list.

Remember, all of this doesn't have to be and can't be done
all at once. Making amends is a slow, gradual process.

Big Book Promises

> From page 83 (line 29) to page 84 (line 11), the Big Book lists the wonderful things that will happen to you as you carefully work these first Nine Steps. Read those promises again now.

List at least five of the promises below, and describe how each of them is beginning to come true in your life. You may need to come back to this page as time goes on to fill in more examples of how your life is improving. If you wish to write more, use a separate sheet of paper.

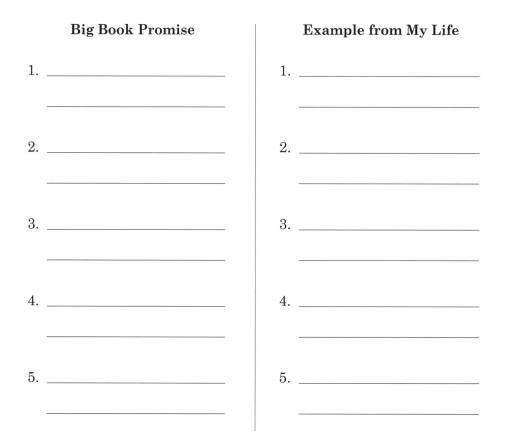

Big Book Promise

1. _____

   _____

2. _____

   _____

3. _____

   _____

4. _____

   _____

5. _____

   _____

Example from My Life

1. _____

   _____

2. _____

   _____

3. _____

   _____

4. _____

   _____

5. _____

   _____

My Tenth Step

Here is the Tenth Step in the AA Twelve Step program:

**"Continued to take personal inventory and when
we were wrong promptly admitted it."**

In Step Ten you'll continue to take personal inventory. The purpose of doing this is so you can continue to grow spiritually. It's not possible to just stay the same, and this is especially true for alcoholics and other addicts. Unless you move forward, you'll slip backward toward the insanity of the illness of the mind—the obsession with the idea that you can safely drink or use again. If this idea is left unchallenged, you'll surely revert to your disease and progression toward death.

It should be pretty obvious from all of this that moving ahead spiritually is essential to recovery. By working Step Ten on a daily basis, you'll also be working Steps Four through Nine each day for the rest of your life. This is how you keep yourself spiritually fit and growing in recovery.

> Now stop and read from page 84, line 16 to page 85, line 23, in your Big Book.

Exercise 1
What the Big Book Says about Step Ten

There are several key ideas in the Big Book's description of Step Ten. Use your own words to tell what the phrases from the Big Book that appear on the next page might mean in your life.

Duplicating this page is illegal. Do not copy this material without written permission from the publisher.

23

"We have entered the world of the Spirit."

"We have ceased fighting anything or anyone."

"What we really have is a daily reprieve contingent on the maintenance of our spiritual condition."

Exercise 2
Nine Questions to Help You Work Step Ten

The "personal inventory" of Step Ten need not be a written one, but perhaps the following questions might help you direct and organize your daily thoughts and reflections in a more meaningful way.

Use the following questions to look at the past twenty-four hours. Briefly fill in your responses to each question either in your mind or in this workbook.

1. How may I have harmed myself or someone else today?

2. Which of my character defects caused me to do those harmful things?

3. How was I selfish, dishonest, resentful, or fearful?

4. Did I ask my Higher Power to remove my selfishness, dishonesty, resentment, and fear as soon as I was aware of them?

☐ Yes   ☐ No

What is left for my Higher Power to remove?

5. Did I admit my mistakes promptly and make amends?

☐ Yes   ☐ No

What do I still need to take care of?

6. How often during the day was I feeling gratitude, and how often was I feeling self-pity?

7. What good did I do today?

8. How was I loving and compassionate?

9. Who did I help today and how?

Exercise 3

"Thy Will (Not Mine) Be Done"

The Big Book says on page 85, lines 18–19, that each day alcoholics "must carry the vision of God's will into all of [their] activities." To express this thought, write out the short prayer on page 85, lines 19–20 of the Big Book, or write a similar prayer in your own words.

Following the prayer on page 85, lines 19–20, the Big Book says that "we can exercise our will power along this line all we wish. It is the proper use of will." This means that your Higher Power— God *as you understand God*—will help with all areas of your life.

The main areas of life appear on the pie shape that follows. These are the things that take time, energy, and attention in the lives of most people. We'll call it the Better-Life Pie—a life free from an obsession with alcohol and other drugs.

On each slice of the Better-Life Pie, draw a picture or describe in a few words how working Steps One through Ten has made your life without alcohol or other drugs saner, happier, freer, and more productive.

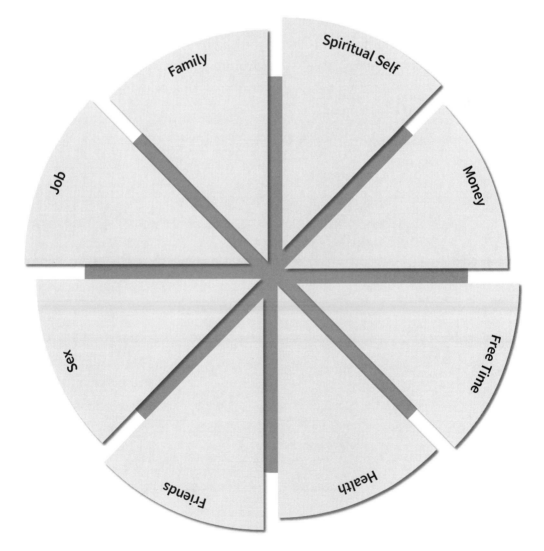

Duplicating this page is illegal. Do not copy this material without written permission from the publisher.

My Tenth Step   27

Celebrate!

You are living a life without alcohol or other drugs, a life that is better in many ways. You are no longer ruled by the obsession to drink or use. You've regained sanity and begun to grow in the *fourth dimension of living: the dimension of the spirit*. It's time to celebrate! Do you feel like you deserve a celebration? If not, what's still blocking your good feelings about yourself and your Twelve Step program? What Steps do you need to rework to remove those blocks?

When you're ready to celebrate, what kind of celebration would you like to have? It doesn't have to be a party or involve a lot of people—it can be anything you want it to be, according to your mood or personality. Who else might be there? What would make it special for you? Describe your celebration below in words or with a drawing. Then go ahead, and make it happen!

My Eleventh Step

Step Eleven is about staying in regular contact with your Higher Power. It's about knowing your Higher Power's will so you'll know what to do in any situation. And Step Eleven tells you exactly how to do this—through prayer and meditation.

Here is the Eleventh Step in the AA Twelve Step program:

"Sought through prayer and meditation to improve our conscious contact with God *as we understood Him,** praying only for knowledge of His will for us and the power to carry that out."

> Before continuing, open your Big Book to page 85, line 24, and read to the end of chapter 6 on page 88.

At first, many people draw a blank or come up with a big question mark when they read about the importance of prayer and meditation. Or maybe they remember the prayer that they used over and over when they were drinking: "God, get me out of this mess, and I swear I'll never do it again!" That's a typical alcoholic's prayer and is pretty much the extent of a lot of alcoholics' and addicts' prayer lives before coming to AA or Narcotics Anonymous. As for meditation, many of us didn't understand what that meant.

It wasn't until we began working the Twelve Steps that most of us saw prayer as a way to receive the will of a Higher Power into our lives. It never occurred to us when drinking or using to even want to receive that will and carry it out. For many of us, prayer was used

---

*Although the Big Book, written in the late 1930s, refers to "God" as "Him," no deliberate gender preference was intended. The words *Her* or simply *God,* depending on your preference, can be substituted for *Him.*

Duplicating this page is illegal. Do not copy this material without written permission from the publisher.

29

to approach God with a list of our petty wants and ask for this thing and that thing, trying to sway God's will to suit our own.

Let's take a minute and, in the exercise on the next page, look at what you think about prayer and meditation.

Exercise 1
Five Questions about Prayer and Meditation

Answer the following questions about prayer and meditation in the spaces provided.

1. What do you think of when you read or hear the word *prayer?*

2. What comes to mind when you think of meditation?

3. How have you used prayer and meditation before?

4. What kind of experience did you have the last time you prayed? Helpful? Unhelpful? Frustrating? Comforting? Describe how you felt.

5. What kind of experience did you have the last time you meditated? Helpful? Unhelpful? Frustrating? Comforting? Describe what you experienced.

The Big Book recognizes that many people may be confused by prayer and meditation and, due to past experiences, may be reluctant to try. On pages 86–88, the Big Book gives you specific ways to overcome your resistance to prayer and meditation. You can teach yourself to do them. Within those directions, prayer is described as a constructive review, a request for inspiration, and humbly asking your Higher Power to make its will known.

Exercise 2
A Guide to Reviewing Your Day

To help you make a constructive review of each day, the Big Book offers specific questions and suggestions on pages 86–88. In the three main areas that follow, you'll be asked to write down these questions and suggestions. Each of these main areas covers one of the three times you'll use prayer and meditation during a twenty-four-hour period: when you go to bed, when you wake up, and during the day. When you're done writing, pick a day and try using this list to structure your thoughts and to answer the questions, either to yourself or by writing them down.

Seven questions to ask when I go to bed. (See the Big Book, page 86, lines 5–18.)

1. _____

2. _____

3. _____

4. _____

5. _____

6. _____

7. _____

When I wake up, what will I be asking God to help me with for the day ahead? (See the Big Book, page 86, line 19 through page 87, line 19.)

1. _____

2. _____

3. _____

4. _____

During the day . . . (See the Big Book, page 87, line 31 through page 88, line 7.)

1. When agitated or doubtful I will _____.

2. I will constantly remind myself _____.

3. and will humbly say to myself as often as I need to,

   "_____."

The following is one prayer some AA members have found useful.

THE PRAYER OF SAINT FRANCIS

"Lord, [you may substitute God, Higher Power, etc. if you wish]
make me a channel of thy peace—that where there is hatred,
I may bring love—that where there is wrong, I may bring the
spirit of forgiveness—that where there is discord, I may bring
harmony—that where there is error, I may bring truth—that where
there is doubt, I may bring faith—that where there is despair,
I may bring hope—that where there are shadows, I may bring
light—that where there is sadness, I may bring joy. Lord, grant
that I may seek rather to comfort than to be comforted—to
understand, than to be understood—to love, than to be loved.
For it is by self-forgetting that one finds. It is by forgiving that one
is forgiven. It is by dying that one awakens to Eternal Life. Amen."

—Reprinted from *Twelve Steps and Twelve Traditions,* page 99

Exercise 3
Prayer and Meditation Log

Recovery is a process that is lived one day at a time. Each of these days should involve prayer and meditation. It may help to use a prayer and meditation schedule or log, especially if you're just starting out. At the top of the next page is an example of a prayer and meditation log.

Prayer and Meditation Log

Date	Place	Time
Thoughts and feelings that block prayer and meditation:		How I can put them aside:

Even though prayer and meditation might sound mystical at first, with practice you'll see a Higher Power's direction for your life. With prayer and meditation in your daily life, inspiration will become more and more a natural part of your thinking.

Here are some other suggestions that might help you get started:

- Plan for prayer and meditation at least fifteen to thirty minutes every day.

- Find a quiet place where you won't be distracted.

- Use a straight-backed chair or sit so your spine is comfortably straight.

- Concentrate on your breathing. It should be slow and regular.

- Be aware of thoughts, feelings, obligations, or other things that block prayer or meditation, and find ways to put them aside or let them pass. (Remember, you are removing obstacles to a Higher Power, which is within all of us.)

- Use affirmations, prayers, or other meditative writings that have been helpful to you in the past.

- Use other resources recommended by your sponsor and by other people in your Twelve Step group whom you trust.

When you've worked the Twelve Step program as it's been described so far, you've made it through the first eleven Steps, and you've had the Big Book's biggest promise fulfilled in your life: You have had a spiritual awakening.

Step Twelve begins with those words. It is stated as a fact.

Duplicating this page is illegal. Do not copy this material without written permission from the publisher.

35

My Twelfth Step

Here is the Twelfth Step in the AA Twelve Step program:

"Having had a spiritual awakening as the result of these steps, we tried to carry this message to alcoholics, and to practice these principles in all our affairs."

> Read chapter 7 in the Big Book, "Working with Others," pages 89–103.

Step Twelve begins by promising you that if you apply the previous eleven Steps in your life and use the kit of simple spiritual tools the Big Book provides, you will have a spiritual awakening. Not "might have" or "should have" or "will probably have"—but *WILL HAVE*.

In Appendix II of the Big Book (pages 569–570) [pages 567–568, 4th ed.], we learn that a spiritual awakening is a "personality change sufficient to bring about recovery from alcoholism." Writing about Step Twelve in *Twelve Steps and Twelve Traditions*, Bill W. describes three things almost all spiritual awakenings have in common:

1. You are able to see and feel things you could never see and feel before.

2. You know things you have never known before.

3. You are able to do things you could never do before.

Duplicating this page is illegal. Do not copy this material without written permission from the publisher.

My Twelfth Step **37**

If you've carefully worked through the first eleven Steps, you can do, feel, and believe things you haven't been able to before. What are some of those things? Draw a picture or describe in words below.

DO

FEEL

BELIEVE

So now that you've had a spiritual awakening as a result of these Steps, what are you supposed to do? The second part of Step Twelve says the message should be carried to other alcoholics and practiced in all your affairs. But what is the message that you should bring to other alcoholics and addicts who still suffer?

The only real message you're qualified to give is that *you have had a spiritual awakening as the result of these Steps.* You can help alcoholics and addicts when no one else can. You are an expert on the disease you're recovering from. And now you have a strong message of hope to carry.

A Higher Power very seldom talks to people directly, but usually works through others. By carrying the message of recovery and spiritual awakening to those still suffering from alcoholism and other drug addictions, you have the chance to help others save their lives. The primary reason you carry the message is that this is how you will stay clean and sober yourself.

Carrying the Message

Think about times you've unselfishly helped others in the past, with no strings attached. How did you feel about yourself?

How will seeking these kinds of experiences by carrying the message help keep you clean and sober?

Chapter 7 of the Big Book offers many suggestions for carrying the message of recovery to others who still suffer. There are some other suggestions that might be helpful as well:

1. If at all possible, go with someone else. It can be dangerous to go alone, especially if you're at all unsure about your own sobriety.

2. Do not talk to someone who doesn't want help. Remember, the message is given through attraction, not promotion.

3. Tell your story in a simple, straightforward way:

   - What it was like (your drinking or using history)

   - What happened (hitting bottom and later experiencing a spiritual awakening)

   - What it's like now (how your life is different clean and sober)

Most of the time, you'll work Step Twelve in your local AA or other Twelve Step meeting. Your commitment to being part of a fellowship, to taking part in meetings, will bring your message of experience, strength, and hope to others as they bring it to you. You are telling others this program works every time you show up at a meeting clean and sober.

At the end of chapter 7 (page 103), the Big Book repeats its message of tolerance. To preach, show intolerance, or condemn will not help anyone. The decision to get sober belongs to each person.

Conclusion

The Big Book reminds us that we are all imperfect human beings, that the Twelve Steps are for guidance and not for 100-percent-perfect obedience. Your claim can be to spiritual progress, not spiritual perfection.

If you make a genuine, honest, and sincere effort to follow the program of recovery in the Big Book to the best of your ability, you will have all the tools you need.

- In Steps One, Two, and Three, you abandon yourself to a Higher Power—God as you understand God.

- In Steps Four, Five, Six, and Seven, you admit your faults to a Higher Power, to yourself, and to your fellow human beings.

- In Steps Eight and Nine, you clear away the wreckage of the past.

- In Steps Ten, Eleven, and Twelve you give freely of what you have found.

Chapters 8, 9, and 10 in the Big Book offer guidance for spouses, family members, and employers. Read and use this information as you need it. The personal stories in the three sections after page 164 will offer confirmation and inspiration for making the Big Book's suggestions your design for living. Finally, read chapter 11, "A Vision for You," and pay special attention to the final two paragraphs on page 164.

You have always been a part of the fellowship of the Spirit. May this program help you to know it so that your life is a journey down the Road of Happy Destiny.

Duplicating this page is illegal. Do not copy this material without written permission from the publisher.

41

The Twelve Steps of Alcoholics Anonymous*

1. We admitted we were powerless over alcohol—that our lives had become unmanageable.

2. Came to believe that a Power greater than ourselves could restore us to sanity.

3. Made a decision to turn our will and our lives over to the care of God *as we understood Him.*

4. Made a searching and fearless moral inventory of ourselves.

5. Admitted to God, to ourselves, and to another human being the exact nature of our wrongs.

6. Were entirely ready to have God remove all these defects of character.

7. Humbly asked Him to remove our shortcomings.

8. Made a list of all persons we had harmed, and became willing to make amends to them all.

9. Made direct amends to such people wherever possible, except when to do so would injure them or others.

10. Continued to take personal inventory and when we were wrong promptly admitted it.

11. Sought through prayer and meditation to improve our conscious contact with God *as we understood Him,* praying only for knowledge of His will for us and the power to carry that out.

12. Having had a spiritual awakening as the result of these steps, we tried to carry this message to alcoholics, and to practice these principles in all our affairs.

---

*The Twelve Steps of AA are taken from *Alcoholics Anonymous,* 3rd and 4th editions, published by A.A. World Services, Inc., New York, N.Y., 59–60. Reprinted with permission of A.A. World Services, Inc.

The Twelve Traditions of Alcoholics Anonymous*

1. Our common welfare should come first; personal recovery depends upon A.A. unity.

2. For our group purpose there is but one ultimate authority—a loving God as He may express Himself in our group conscience. Our leaders are but trusted servants; they do not govern.

3. The only requirement for A.A. membership is a desire to stop drinking.

4. Each group should be autonomous except in matters affecting other groups or A.A. as a whole.

5. Each group has but one primary purpose—to carry its message to the alcoholic who still suffers.

6. An A.A. group ought never endorse, finance or lend the A.A. name to any related facility or outside enterprise, lest problems of money, property and prestige divert us from our primary purpose.

7. Every A.A. group ought to be fully self-supporting, declining outside contributions.

8. Alcoholics Anonymous should remain forever nonprofessional, but our service centers may employ special workers.

9. A.A., as such, ought never be organized; but we may create service boards or committees directly responsible to those they serve.

10. Alcoholics Anonymous has no opinion on outside issues; hence the A.A. name ought never be drawn into public controversy.

11. Our public relations policy is based on attraction rather than promotion; we need always maintain personal anonymity at the level of press, radio, and films.

12. Anonymity is the spiritual foundation of all our Traditions, ever reminding us to place principles before personalities.

---

*The Twelve Traditions of AA are taken from *Alcoholics Anonymous,* 3rd ed., published by A.A. World Services, Inc., New York, NY, 564 [page 562, 4th ed.]. Reprinted with permission of A.A. World Services, Inc.

About the Authors

Writers and educators James and Joanne Hubal bring to their work years of training and experience in various areas of expertise, including the field of addiction treatment. Joanne Hubal has been a writer, teacher, and cartoonist. She specializes in education and humor writing. James Hubal has developed and modified curriculum materials for schools throughout the country.

Since they were first published in 1991, the Hubals' *Living With...* workbooks, adapted from the material written in *A Program for You: A Guide to the Big Book's Design for Living,* have helped hundreds of thousands of recovering people engage and incorporate the Twelve Steps in their lives of healing and recovery.

About Hazelden Publishing

As part of the Hazelden Betty Ford Foundation, Hazelden Publishing offers both cutting-edge educational resources and inspirational books. Our print and digital works help guide individuals in treatment and recovery, and their loved ones. Professionals who work to prevent and treat addiction also turn to Hazelden Publishing for evidence-based curricula; digital content solutions; and videos for use in schools, treatment and correctional programs, and community settings. We also offer training for implementation of our curricula.

Through published and digital works, Hazelden Publishing extends the reach of healing and hope to individuals, families, and communities affected by addiction and related issues.

For more information about Hazelden publications,
please call **800-328-9000**
or visit us online at **hazelden.org/bookstore**.

Also in This Series

A Program for You: A Guide to the Big Book's Design for Living

This celebration of the basic text of Twelve Step recovery breathes new life into the Big Book's timeless wisdom. Thoroughly annotated, written with down-to-earth humor and simplicity, and providing a contemporary context for understanding, *A Program for You* helps us experience the same path of renewal that Bill W. and the first one hundred AA members did.

Item 5122 · 192 pages

Living with Your Higher Power: A Workbook for Steps 1–3

This workbook features information to reinforce important points in *A Program for You* and includes exercises for self-examination and disclosure. Clear discussions of Steps 1–3 and probing questions offer a guide to personal insight and reflection

Item 5421 · 52 pages

Living with Yourself: A Workbook for Steps 4–7

This workbook features information to reinforce important points in *A Program for You* and includes exercises for self-examination and disclosure. Clear discussions of Steps 4–7 and probing questions offer a guide to personal insight and reflection.

Item 5422 · 64 pages

Other Titles That May Interest You

A Gentle Path through the Twelve Steps
By Patrick Carnes

Renowned addiction expert and best-selling author Patrick Carnes, PhD, brings readers a personal portal to the wisdom of the Twelve Steps.

Item 2558 · 340 pages

Twelve Step Pamphlet Collection

Used by patients in recovery centers throughout the nation, these easy-to-read editions are a sure way to gain a basic, and yet thorough, understanding of the significance of each Step.

Item 1455 · 12 Pamphlets

Twenty-Four Hours a Day

A mainstay in recovery literature, "the little black book—*Twenty-Four Hours a Day*"—is the first and foremost meditation book for anyone practicing the Twelve Steps of AA. Millions of copies sold.

Item 1050 · 400 pages

Coming Soon

How We Heal

A diverse and inclusive meditation book for people with co-occurring sexual trauma and substance use disorders, this unique title brings together many individual voices to create a symphony of survivors all saying the same thing: you are not alone.